Early Retirement Success Secrets!

I0486139

Retirement

The Ultimate Retirement Planning Guide To Get Out Of Debt, Create Passive Income To Quit Your Day Job, And Travel The World!

Mick McPherson

STOP!!! Before you read any further....Would you like to know the Success Secrets of how to make Passive Income Online?

If your answer is yes, then you are not alone. Thousands of people are looking for the secret to learning how to create their own online passive income style business.

If you have been searching for these answers without much luck, you are in the right place!

Because I want to make sure to give you as much value as possible for purchasing this book, right now for a limited time you can get 3 incredible bonuses for free.

At the end of this book I describe all 3 bonuses. You can access them at the end. But for those of you that want to grab your bonuses right now. See below.

Just Go Here For Free Instant Access:

www.OperationAwesomeLife.com/FreeBonuses

Legal Notice

Disclaimer Notice

Table Of Contents

Introduction

I want to thank you and congratulate you for purchasing the book, *"Retirement: Early Retirement Success Secrets! - The Ultimate Retirement Planning Guide To Get Out Of Debt, Create Passive Income To Quit Your Day Job, And Travel The World!"*.

This "Retirement" book contains proven steps and strategies on how to plan out your life after pursuing a career job. This is of course a significant matter most especially if you want your retirement years to be enjoyable, comfortable, and debt-free. Actually, you don't have to stop making money when this time comes. Many of those who have wisely invested their money on profitable ventures and passive income sources have succeeded in their goals. This is to ensure that their pension is not their only source of income. Even a retired individual could make a lot of money from passive income and use it to enjoy the rest of his life after retirement.

It all comes down to careful planning and wise use of resources when they were still young or near the age of retirement. Unfortunately, not all of us know the right way around this matter. There are lots of risks in investments. There are many complicated things that one should deal with in order to effectively get out of debt. Luckily, the cause is not yet lost. Retiring happy and with enough money to do what you want is possible.

This book will guide you with the basics of planning for your retirement, what to do with your money, how to start with debt management, and how to get the most out of your retirement years.

Don't worry, there is nothing complicated presented on the pages of this book. Everything has been simplified so that you can immediately understand the concepts that need to be learned and the things that need to be done. By going through the ten chapters of this book, you'll be armed with the knowledge that will make your retirement a better one.

Thanks again for purchasing this book, I hope you enjoy it!

Chapter 1: How To Set A Budget For Retirement

Most probably, you are aware of why and how you must allocate what you are earning right now. Yes, we are talking about your income and all the money that you might have saved up. Budgeting for retirement purposes is as important as budgeting while you're actively working today. This is what a lot of people don't realize early.

Of course, it is very important that you realize this now. There is a common notion that when an individual retires, he or she will have less to spend on. Yes, this may be correct but only in a partial way. You might not spend as much on daily travel expenses, coffee, or lunch but there will be a catch here. This is the fact that there will always be things that need to be paid. There are monthly bills, needs for leisure, and medical expenses that might be more regular than what you might expect.

The common mistake that people make is to think that when they retire, they have enough money. Yes, the monthly pension you will get is fixed. It will come on time. However, there is a factor that could lead you to go broke halfway through the month. This is your spending behavior. Budgeting is the best way for you to make sure that you will be prepared for the eventualities that a retired life could give.

By creating budget for your retirement, you are putting yourself in control of the investments that you can make for your future life. You can make smart choices like sacrificing some things in order to ensure that you can travel, do your dream hobbies, or even buy that nice vacation house that you've always wanted. So, it is difficult to create your retirement budget? Absolutely not!

Let us get started by enumerating the things you'll need for this matter. Prepare the following things:

- Your bank account and credit card statements for half a year.
- Your pay slips for the last two months. (Include your spouse's pay slip if you are married.)
- Your tax documents for the previous year.
- Highlighting pens.

Now that you have all the materials needed, just follow the procedure as presented below:

1. Create a list of your monthly payables or obligations. To make sure that you include everything, there are three categories that must be created. These include the essentials, non-essentials, and those required expenses that are not paid on a monthly basis but could come up once or twice in a year.
2. Plan out your expenses for health care services. Come up with researched data before and after retirement.
3. Create a list that is meant for expenses that can be classified as optional or flexible. Examples include travel, hobbies, and amusement.
4. You and your spouse should write a reflection of how you want your retired life to end up. By doing this, you will have an idea of what part of your budget to adjust and what to keep intact in order to achieve your "dream retired life". Modify items on your fixed and optional expenses list.
5. Separately compute for the total fixed and optional expenses.
6. Compare your monthly income with the expenses. How much of it will go to fixed and optional expenses?
7. If you want to spend much time on hobbies and fun, you should find ways to reduce the amount of your fixed expenses. This is the general rule of budgeting for a fun retirement.

By doing the steps mentioned above, you will have a clearer idea on what your retirement life would turn out to be. Of course, you are in complete control over this matter. Use your newly acquired budgeting knowledge to ensure that you will make right decisions about income, investments, and expenditures today.

Turn to the next chapter to see what type of investments you should go for.

Chapter 2: Profitable Retirement Investments

People save up their money today so that they would have something to spend later in their life. While the idea here is good, there is a better thing that could be done. Yes, we are talking about making your saved money earn more money. A couple of decades back, not many people are willing to risk their hard earned retirement money on such things. However, with the growth of the economy and stories about successful retirement money investments making the news, there is an observable paradigm shift.

Options for those who are planning to get involved in retirement investments have increased. There are investments that are proven to yield guaranteed amounts of profits. Would you be interested in seeing your money grow? Of course this is what all of us would be interested in!

To invest means to put your money in the right places. On this matter, the following options should be considered:

1. **Employer-offered retirement plan**. Examples include the popular 401 (k) and 401 (b). This is a wise way of investing your money because while it is in these plans, income is generated. The best thing here is that you can enjoy tax advantages on the income made, on the premiums, or on the money that you will withdraw when you retire. Of course, you have to choose the right type of plan in order to enjoy a specific tax advantage.
2. **Individual Retirement Account (IRA)**. This can be added to your retirement plan. There are also tax advantages here. IRA accounts and the money in there could be used for additional investments that would also yield tax advantages. The use of IRA money in precious metals and real estate investment is fast gaining popularity now because of guaranteed and solid profits.

3. **Traditional Investment Accounts**. These are regular investment accounts which don't offer the tax advantage feature. However, the best thing about this is that you will never be stopped by investment amount caps. The first two items mentioned above might be profitable but there are maximum investment amounts that are implemented. You can invest profitably in cash, stocks, and bonds. The best way to cover it all is to invest in a mutual fund.

Whatever your investment decision may be, the best advice that you can follow is to always do your research first. Find out about the pros and cons of each of the options presented above. Make your final decision based on your goals, the money that you have, and the level of risk that you are willing to take. Remember that you will put your precious retirement money on the line. Make hasty decisions and you will surely end up losing a lot. However, if you will make informed decisions, the monetary rewards will always be big and worth all the risk you will take.

Chapter 3: Steps To Get Out Of Debt

If you doubt the decision to invest your retirement money in profitable ventures today, the most likely reason is that you are still deep in debt. If you are aiming for an enjoyable retirement, you've got to figure a way out of debts.

Actually, there are proven steps on how you can manage getting out of debts. There are many online information sources that could give you varied ideas about this matter. The simplest yet most effective steps have been outlined below:

STEP 1: Break the cycle of debt by establishing an emergency fund. Financial planning experts are recommending that you stash away as much $1000 on this emergency fund. When emergency needs arise, this fund can be used while you are working to pay off old debts and preventing new ones from being made.

STEP 2: Get motivated to pay off debts. List your debts in an order of increasing amounts (lowest amounts listed first). Cross out those little debts that you manage to pay. This creates a psychological effect of "winning" which motivates an individual to aim for better results. As you see your debts getting paid off one by one, you feel pumped up to finish it all.

STEP 3: Establish a "lifeline savings account". This is separate from your emergency fund. This is where you will put your extra income or savings. How much should you save? Think about how much money you will need in a span of 2 to 3 months if you got fired from a job or lost your current business. This will be the basis of how much you should target to put into your "lifeline savings account"

STEP 4: Create a monthly budget and follow it strictly. Manage what you have and don't go beyond your means. Yes, this might mean giving up some personal pleasures like going to the movies or buying the latest gadgets that appear on your favorite online shopping site. The sacrifices are all temporary. Remember that when you finally settle all of your debts, these pleasures that you missed could all be enjoyed.

STEP 5: **Declare your intent to avoid getting into more debts**. You can do this by consciously avoiding that urge to spend what you don't have yet. Remind yourself that you need to pay off your current debts and that you don't need any new ones. Kill off the temptation to fund your lifestyle with money that you will borrow.

STEP 6: **Supplement your current income**: Some online sites will recommend debt consolidation. While this is a wise move, it will still involve borrowing money to pay off loans. The best way to tip the scale is to let more money in through income supplementation. By trimming down your current expenses and earning additional money, getting out of debt will be easier.

The steps mentioned above should help you get on the right track when it comes on your aim to get out of debt. However, the last step was not really that clear when it comes to what you can specifically do. Yes, you should supplement your income but in what way? The next chapter should answer this easily.

Chapter 4: Tips For Creating Passive Income

If you are employed full-time, it is very obvious that you'll find a second or third job too complicated to handle. Putting your need for an extra income in consideration, the best solution is all about creating a passive income stream. Passive income sources require less hands-on involvement which is a big advantage for your situation.

If you are looking for the best passive ways to make money, the following ways are considered "hot items".

- **Affiliate marketing**: This means being the bridge between a seller and a buyer. Basically, you will endorse the product of a seller on your website. There is no need to work on marketing and sales talk. All that you have to do is to set up a website and place there the affiliate links of products that you want to promote. The catch here is that you need to set up a website that really drives in traffic or visitors. Income through commissions that you can make will be of considerable amount provided you have met all the requirements of a good affiliate marketing setup.
- **Buy and sell**: We are talking about online sales here. You can have someone do the sales activity on your behalf while you supply the materials needed.
- **Royalties**: If you have some talents or skills that could help you come up with a unique product, this could be a source of passive income. Song writers, painters, sculptors, and a lot of creative artists are known to make passive money successfully. If you can write e-books, a copy could continually sell online once published.
- **Network marketing**: This would require work at the start but once you already become a leader and there are people working under your network, passive income earning will not be a problem anymore. Visit online sites that offer MLM opportunities and examine the fine print before you invest in money.

- **Investments managed by fund managers**: If your interest is in stocks, bonds, and other similar things, you can just let a professional fund manager take care of things for you. Yes, there are lots of these professionals out there today. Of course, you'll have to deal with their regular professional fees but this is something that you can recover when income starts coming in.

The ways of making passive income as presented will be very tempting for a lot of individuals to get engaged in. However, it should be noted that there are no overnight successes that could be gained from any of those things. Remember the following tips when planning to establish a passive income stream:

- ✓ Always put research first on your to-do list. It will verify that your decision is wise and profitable enough.
- ✓ Don't put all of your money in only one form of passive income source.
- ✓ Consider carefully the kind of competition that you will encounter.
- ✓ If you have a product that was creatively conceptualized, publish or patent it.
- ✓ Outsourcing of services when it comes to creating unique products will give you a lot of benefits.
- ✓ Be prepared to put up a website that is optimized for online business and passive income streaming.

Creating a passive income is something that is doable but requires a lot of wise decision making at the start. Use the information presented on this chapter to plan out your passive income source for the future.

Chapter 5: Quit Your Day Job And Start An Online Business

It is a normal thing for extra income sources to flourish and develop into a full-blown business. When conditions are good, you could even quit your day job and focus on the business that you are running. These days, the profitability of online businesses is gaining a lot of attention. Of course, we need to put in a considerable amount of effort, skills, and time on the whole matter.

Many online articles advise against quitting a day job just to focus on an online business. The authors of these articles are aware of the volatility of the e-commerce world and are probably talking about what could happen when things go south on an investment or business. Those who see their online ventures fail would commonly go crawling back to their day jobs.

The way to prevent this from happening is to make sure that you have a solid and sustainable business and that the transition between the employed and entrepreneur's life goes smoothly. There are some steps that should be taken when it comes to this. These are as follows:

1. **Establish a "transition savings fund"**. The money that would be saved on this fund should be enough to cover your daily expenses for at least six months.
2. **Evaluate the kind of income that you'll need in order to stay in self-employed status**. Would this be enough to cover your expenses and give you room for other needs?
3. **Evaluate the potentials of your business**. It should be able to give you a boosted income amount when you go full-time on it. If the business cannot be scaled up in terms of profits you will earn, it isn't worth it to quit your day job and go full-time on it.

Now that you are aware of the steps to take to effectively go through the income transition mentioned above, it is time to look at what types of ventures should be given attention. In terms of profitability and capacity to replace a day job, the following online businesses are the best ones to pursue:

- App development
- Online instruction
- Online selling
- Technical support service
- Online writing/editing/e-book authoring
- Health and nutrition coaching
- Affiliate marketing
- Web designing
- Consultancy services for varied fields (SEO, social media, real estate, etc.)
- Specialized retailing
- Commercial blogging

The types of profitable online businesses that you can pick and get involved in are not limited to the ones listed above. It would be best if you will do your research and see which ones will really match your skills, the current needs in the market, and the profit level that you want.

Chapter 6: How To Travel The World On A Budget

Do you need to be a millionaire to travel around the world? The answer here is no. While it is very obvious that you will spend considerable amounts of money on such trips, there are ways to cut down costs. In the process, you can also ensure that your trip will stay as fun as it should be.

The following tips should guide you on what to do for this matter:

- Stay in hostels and apartments instead of booking expensive hotel rooms. This mode of arranging your accommodation could cut down your expenses a lot.
- Shop for food from grocery stores and public shops. Vending machines, specialty shops, and souvenir stores can charge a lot for these items.
- Carry a reusable drinking bottle when you travel. Most of the time, tap water from each destination you will visit will be safe to drink. Many businesses charge a lot on bottled water since they know that travelers need it much.
- Buy food items and beverages in bulk. Buying little by little while you are on the road will lead to more expenses.
- Always do your research when it comes to airfare and transportation fees. There are cheap options that could offer the same benefits for a traveler like you.
- Stick to public means of transportation when you want to save a lot of money. While taxis are convenient, they usually charge outrageously high fare rates when you are an obvious tourist.
- A swish knife can eliminate your need to buy tools like scissors, screw drivers, compass, and other similar things while on the road. Buy one before you pack up for the trip.
- Book all the flights, transportation, and accommodation that you will need ahead of time. This way, you are most likely to be entitled for discounts, special offers, and freebies. Bookings that are made on the spot are more expensive and time consuming.

- Ask for discounts that you might qualify for. Many travel booking agencies, hotels, restaurants, and other establishments all over the world give such discounts to retired individuals, their young travel companions, and even to students.

As you can see, it is not really impossible to travel around the world on a budget. With proper research, planning, and the use of your social skills in dealing with people, good deals are easy to get. Do your bookings and see to it that you really know your destinations well.

Chapter 7: Importance Of Goal Setting

What are your plans once you have retired? The most common answer here is all about traveling. While there is nothing wrong in planning to hit the road and see the world, there should be more concrete plans other than traveling. What are you going to do after you have come home from those trips? This is where you will realize that retirement is more than just going to places that you have always dreamed of visiting.

It is in here where the importance of goal setting during the process of planning for retirement could be seen. Yes, a clear vision of what you want should be there but you should include long term plans on your list. A world tour could last for a couple of months. Of course, you will live much longer than this. It is a good idea to have a more concrete plan of what you are going to do with the money that you have accumulated and the free time that have just been made available for you.

There is nothing wrong in planning for retirement as early as possible. Of course, you can also make those plans if you are just months away from retiring. The important thing is that you should have a list of what to do in order to have a happy and fulfilled retired life. Goal setting is not really complicated. Start by answering some questions that are relevant to your retirement. These questions include the following:

- ✓ **What is your most ideal retirement vision?** This question lets you identify those things that really matter to you. By answering this, you are given the opportunity to see what to prioritize when preparing for retirement.
- ✓ **What are included in your retirement to-do list?** You should come up with a list of all the things that you want to do when you retire. It will make you realize that retirement signals freedom to do a lot of things. Of course, you can include your plan to travel on this list.

✓ ***What things about your current work will you miss the most?*** This question will make you realize that some of your plans for retirement should include activities that involve socializing with or being around people.

Using the answers that you will give for the questions above, create a goals matrix that include very specific items. Separate what you want and need to do. With this matrix of goals around, you'll have a more solid retirement life to look forward to.

Chapter 8: Early Retirement Mistakes To Avoid

Surely, you have seen those online articles today that mention about the trend of early retirement among the employed sector. Yes, we want to retire early and really experience how it feels to enjoy spending the money that we have worked so hard to save up. However, this eagerness to bite the offer for early retirement could easily lead to regrettable circumstances.

The mere fact that your attention has been grabbed by the thought of early retirement means that you are prone to make some very common mistakes that others before you already committed. There is nothing wrong in retiring early but you should make sure that you don't commit the following mistakes:

- **Not controlling spending habits**. Yes, you might be tempted to make those lump sum withdrawals but you must think of the years ahead. Life expectancy has improved greatly today due to medical breakthroughs and technologies. If you will retire early, see to it that your withdrawals are at 3% or less.
- **Giving up on earning on the side**. This may be due to the fact that you could end up being overconfident about the money you are expecting. Since you retired early, you still have some skills that could be used to augment what you will get from your pension. You should not be contented on having only a single income stream during your retired life.
- **Claiming social security benefits too soon**. You or your spouse should opt to delay claiming social security benefits. This strategy, as seen by many financial experts, has made it possible for retired couples to make their money last longer.
- **Setting aside plans for future medical needs**. Just because you feel strong today doesn't mean that you'll stay in that condition for the years to come. Those who retire

early should be the ones to really pay attention to investing on medical insurance and service solutions for the future.

- **Involvement in low risk investments**. The most common turnout on this scenario is that you will end up with less money than you expect when the actual retirement age comes.

The mistakes mentioned above are just some of the most common ones that you are likely to commit. Now that you have become aware of each of those things, go to the next step which is a careful planning of that early retirement you are dreaming of doing. Weigh things before making that final decision to finally retire.

Chapter 9: Pursuing Your Dreams And Life Passions

Do you believe that retirement is your ticket to finally start pursuing those dreams and life passions? Many years ago, a lot of people believed in this notion. However, you should realize that there is no more reason to wait for retirement for you to be able to do all those things. Of course, upon retirement, you'll have a significant amount of money to spend. However, will this be all that you would need in order to do those things that you are dreaming about?

Take for example those adventure-filled travels that you want to embark on. If you will wait until you have reached 65 and older before you do this, you really can't do a lot. Will you still have the stamina to climb those steep trails in the mountains? Can your body take the pressure of extreme sports? Will you be able to keep up with your trip buddies when you go country hiking? These are just some of the best examples of why you shouldn't delay pursuing your dreams and passions anymore.

It is all about aiming to achieve that sense of fulfillment and happiness before you even retire. Nobody could guarantee that when you reach retirement age, your health will still be in its prime levels. A retired life should be focused on enjoying what you have accomplished and done during your younger years. This makes more sense most especially when you really envision the later part of your life as peaceful, contented, and not having any regrets about things.

Don't let your current job hold you back from doing what you really love. If you have been working with your company for a long time already, use your leave or vacation privileges. If this isn't possible, find organizations or groups of people who might be sharing the same passion and dreams as you are. Seek advice on how you could pursue your dreams at this point in your life. Learn about success stories of people and pick lessons from it which you can apply for your situation.

When you are near retirement, there is a possibility that you have already made significant investments. If this is the case, use this as a motivation that you can really start pursuing those dreams and life passions without fear of losing your current job.

There is no doubt that retirement is still a key for you to achieve a significant amount of freedom to do what you want. However, there will barriers or hindrances that are already present when this time of your life comes. Take this advice: don't wait until retirement for you to do those things that you really love. Act now and attain a good level of self-fulfillment!

Chapter 10: Determine What You Want And How Much Money You Will Need

Now that we are on the last chapter of this book, you should already have a clear idea about the things that you want when you retire. Of course, you want the first year of your retirement to be all about activities that will lead you to enjoyment of saved up money. However, after all the smokes of festivities have cleared up, you'll surely want a comfortable retired life where you get by effortlessly each day.

If this is what you really want, you'll know how much money will be needed in order to get it. In short, you'll be asking yourself the question of how much money you'd need in order to retire happy and contented. Retirement planning and consultancy experts are being tapped by many would-be-retirees today. However, you can really figure things out even when they are not around.

Different financial experts will be seen and heard saying different things about how much money you should have saved up when you already have plans to retire. One expert says that if you are aged 65, you should have saved up at least 11 times of your annual income. Another one is saying that your savings should be at least 33 times above your expected expenses for the first year of your retirement.

Now, even if the statements differ, a common ground can be established. These experts are merely trying to say that a considerable amount of savings is needed before you can expect a comfortable retirement. Financial planning for retirement should be done at this stage. If you can still remember the retirement planning lesson you got in Chapter 1, the planning that you will do here will be similar.

There are online calculators that can help in your financial planning for retirement. Make sure that you are able to include factors such as life expectancy, inflation, future costs of medical services, nature of investments, and rate of savings. The use of these online calculators is commonly for free and comes with no obligations from the company that provides it. Through the computations that will be laid out, you will have a clearer idea if what you have is really enough for what you want when you retire.

Don't worry if you see that there are still issues to resolve. You still have time to prepare and a lot of your options can be found on the previous chapters of this book. Go through each section and see what course of action you can take in order to have enough for retirement.

So, now you have all the information that you need! Plan out your retirement as early as you can by using what you have learned from this book. Good luck and enjoy your life!

Conclusion

Thank you again for purchasing this book on "Retirement: Early Retirement Success Secrets! - The Ultimate Retirement Planning Guide To Get Out Of Debt, Create Passive Income To Quit Your Day Job, And Travel The World!".

I am extremely excited to pass this information along to you, and I am so happy that you now have read and can hopefully implement these strategies going forward.

I hope this book was able to help you understand the complex issues that come with retirement planning and how to come up with practical solutions for each.

The next step is to get started using this information and to hopefully live a contented, happy, and fulfilled retired life!

Please don't be someone who just reads this information and doesn't apply it, the strategies in this book will only benefit you if you use them!

If you know of anyone else that could benefit from the information presented here please inform them of this book.

Finally, if you enjoyed this book and feel it has added value to your life in any way, please take the time to share your thoughts and post a review on Amazon. It'd be greatly appreciated!

Thank you and good luck!

Preview Of:

Ultimate Accelerated Learning Techniques!

Accelerated Learning

Best Accelerated Learning Tips To Improve Memory And Speed Reading, Enhance Intellect And Brain Power, And To Learn More Faster!

Introduction

I want to thank you and congratulate you for purchasing the book, *"Accelerated Learning: Ultimate Accelerated Learning Techniques! - Best Accelerated Learning Tips To Improve Memory And Speed Reading, Enhance Intellect And Brain Power, And To Learn More Faster!"*

This "Accelerated Learning" book contains proven steps and strategies on how to learn things faster using minimal effort. Thanks to the current studies that link the nature of the human brain to the learning process; there are concepts and methodologies that could be used to boost man's capacity to learn more.

While there are already solid educational psychology laws that govern and explain the process of learning in humans, there are researchers who still want to push on into the realms of "hyper learning". Traditional methods of teaching and learning are effective up to this day. However, the advancements in society and technology deem it necessary that the new generation of learners keep up.

There are many approaches to speed up the learning process. This will depend upon the background of the one who is aiming towards it. Psychologists, teachers, neurologists, and even child development experts have different techniques to share when it comes to boosting up the rate of learning within individuals. However, there are aspects on which their approaches meet. This is where the principles of A. L. or Accelerated Learning were born.

Combining different methodologies from different areas of specialization would seem too complicated for an individual aiming to go for self-initiated accelerated learning. This is the reason why this book was conceptualized and put together. Every aspect of accelerated learning will be discussed in the simplest manner possible.

Techniques that are proven to boost memory, improve learning efficiency and effectiveness, condition the brain for learning, develop study habits, and improve overall academic performance are included in this book.

It is hoped that through the use of this e-book, grasping the principles, concepts, and techniques of accelerated learning will be easy for anybody to do.

Thanks again for purchasing this book, I hope you enjoy it!

Chapter 1: Fundamentals Of Accelerated Learning

Accelerated learning or A.L. is currently getting a lot of attention these days. This can be explained by the fact that from a collection of concepts and research-backed principles, a lot of impressive practical applications can be derived out of it. There are many pieces of scientific literature already written about this as of present time. While the explanation about AL may vary according to who is talking, it could be explained in just a simple line. Accelerated learning is the most cutting-edge collection of theories, applications, and strategies that is aimed at boosting the speed and quality of learning. Yes, AL principles are backed up with huge quantities of hard data that were derived from years of research. An individual with a capacity to learn at speeds above the standard figures will have a better shot at achieving career success. There are many organizations and entities in the education and business sectors that have benefited already from the results of accelerated learning programs.

There are education and learning laws and principles currently seen to work just fine for individuals. The thing that separates AL from the traditional methods of learning is that it harnesses the latent capacities of the human brain. Traditional methods leave a lot of room for wasted learning opportunities. AL effectively uses these rooms to maximize the rate of learning that an individual could achieve. The multiple intelligence utilization approach of AL means that the process will include use of physical activities, music, sound, tactile materials, and other related things. By optimizing the environment where a learner is in, more positive results can be achieved.

Based from accelerated learning principles, an optimal environment is one that is:

- **Rooted on positivity** – This is because a positive atmosphere relaxes and stimulates the brain of a learner. An individual will learn best if he or she feels a sense of safety, wholeness, and freedom to enjoy in a specific area or setting.

- **Allows active involvement** – Knowledge is best gained when an individual has a participatory (active) role in a learning scenario. A spectator's (passive) role can reward an individual with knowledge but only to a very limited extent.

- **Gives way to cooperation between learners**: The cooperative learning strategy as used in the current curriculum of educational institutions ensure higher quality of concept and knowledge formation among individuals.

- **Options for learning are varied**: There are many learning styles among individuals. The learner should have the freedom to choose his means and ways to grasp knowledge and skills. Each option should match the learning style of an individual.

- **Offers application of learned knowledge and skills**: This is called learning in context of use. Opportunities that are used in real-life scenarios are remembered better and longer.

- **Results-driven and gives way to more challenges**: Learners are always made aware of their goal which motivates them to boost up their efforts. When an individual has clear goals set right from the start, clear methodologies can also be prepared and followed.

Those who are planning to make use of the accelerated learning system must stick to its seven guiding principles. These are as follows:

Principle #1: Learning process should involve both mind and body.

Principle #2: Learning is all about creation and not absorption.

Principle #3: Learning happens best when there is collaboration.

Principle #4: Learning is a multi-process system.

Principle #5: Learning works through the input-process-feedback cycle.

Principle#6: Learning is a direct result of positively reinforced emotion.

Principle#7: Learning results from the image processing power of the human brain.

If we will look at the bigger picture, accelerated learning is like standard learning shifted to a higher gear. There are unconventional practices that rooted out from the introduction of AL into the normal learning systems we are used to. Examples include the use of classical music in a classroom setting, meditation before reading through lessons, and the use of mnemonic memorization tools.

If you need to learn the methods of this learning system, you are reading the right book. The next chapter will discuss the first and most basic part of the AL system...the human memory. Read on and start your journey towards being an "accelerated learner"!

Thanks for Previewing My Exciting Book Entitled:

"Accelerated Learning: Ultimate Accelerated Learning Techniques! Best Accelerated Learning Tips To Improve Memory And Speed Reading, Enhance Intellect And Brain Power, And To Learn More Faster!"

To purchase this book, simply go to the Amazon Kindle store and simply search:

"ACCELERATED LEARNING"

Then just scroll down until you see my book. You will know it is mine because you will see my name "Mick McPherson" underneath the title.

Alternatively, you can visit my author page on Amazon to see this book and other work I have done. Thanks so much, and please don't forget your free bonuses

DON'T LEAVE YET! - CHECK OUT YOUR FREE BONUSES BELOW!

Free Bonus Offer 1: Get Free Access To The OperationAwesomeLife.com VIP Newsletter!

Free Bonus Offer 2: Get A Free Download Of My Friends Amazing Book "Passive Income" First Chapter!

Free Bonus Offer 3: Get A Free Email Series On Making Money Online When You Join Newsletter!

GET ALL 3 FREE

Once you enter your email address you will immediately get free access to this awesome **VIP NEWSLETTER!**

For a limited time, if you join for free right now, you will also get free access to the first chapter of the awesome book **"PASSIVE INCOME"**!

And, last but definitely not least, if you join the newsletter right now, you also will get a free 10 part email series on **10 SUCCESS SECRETS OF MAKING MONEY ONLINE!**

To claim all 3 of your FREE BONUSES just click below!

Just Go Here for all 3 VIP bonuses!

OperationAwesomeLife.com

www.ingramcontent.com/pod-product-compliance
Lightning Source LLC
Chambersburg PA
CBHW070751180526
45168CB00004B/1583